Christian Spirituality

Living for Jesus every moment

Johnny Armstrong

INVICTUS MANEO PRESS

Centreville, VA

Copyright © 2025 by John M. Armstrong

All rights reserved under International and Pan-American Copyright Conventions. By payment of the required fees, you have been granted the nonexclusive, nontransferable right to access and read the text of this e-book on-screen. No part of this text may be reproduced, transmitted, downloaded, decompiled, reverse-engineered, or stored in or introduced into any information storage and retrieval system, in any form or by any means, whether electronic or mechanical, now known or hereafter invented, without the express written permission of Invictus Maneo Press.

Any Internet addresses (websites, blogs, etc.), authors, and thought leaders referenced in this book are offered as a resource to the reader. They are not intended in any way to be or imply an endorsement on the part of the author or publisher, nor do they vouch for their content.

Scripture quotations are taken from the ESV® Bible (The Holy Bible, English Standard Version®). Copyright © 2001 by Crossway, a publishing ministry of Good News Publishers. Used by permission. All rights reserved.

ISBN: 978-1-7323865-3-2 (paperback)

To all my brothers and sisters in the faith who, like me, need to be encouraged to not lose heart in the daily struggle to stay on the path following Jesus.

Contents

Prologue
.... vii

Chapter 1: The Supernatural Universe (part 1)
.... 1

Chapter 2: The Supernatural Universe (part 2)
.... 11

Chapter 3: In the Spirit's Power
.... 19

Chapter 4: Life in the Church
.... 31

Chapter 5: The Christian and the Law(s)
.... 41

Prologue

The inspiration for this short devotional book is Francis Schaeffer's classic, *True Spirituality: How to Live for Jesus Moment By Moment*, which was originally published in 1971. I have distilled what have been to me the most practically applicable guiding principles from his thoughts into a short book that I hope will encourage readers in their faith journey.

Chapter 1: The Supernatural Universe (part 1)

Let's begin with the following illustration: Think of two chairs set out in front of you. The people who sit in these chairs look at the universe in different ways. We are all sitting in one of these chairs throughout our lives. The first person sits in his or her chair and faces the total reality of the universe, the seen part and the normally unseen part, and consistently sees truth against this backdrop. The Christian sits in that chair, which reflects what emerges from the following passages:

> Romans 8:24 For in this hope we were saved. Now hope that is seen is not hope. For who hopes for what he sees?
>
> Hebrews 11:1 Now faith is the assurance of things hoped for, the conviction of things not seen.
>
> 2 Corinthians 4:18; 5:7 ...as we look not to the things that are seen but to the things that are unseen. For the things that are seen are transient, but the things that are unseen are eternal. ... for we walk by faith, not by sight.

Someone resistant to the idea that the supernatural realm plays a significant role in how life is approached, such as an atheist or an agnostic, sits in another chair. This person sees only the natural part of the universe and interprets truth against that backdrop. These two positions cannot both be true. One is true; one is false. If indeed the universe is nothing but a closed system of purely naturally occurring causes and effects absent any spiritual dimension whatsoever, then to sit in the other chair is to delude oneself. If, however, there are the two halves of reality, then to sit in the naturalist's chair is to be extremely naïve and to misunderstand the universe completely. From the Christian viewpoint, no man has ever been so naïve, nor so ignorant of the universe, as a materialist.

However, living as a Christian in the manner taught and exemplified by Christ and the apostles as described in the New Testament requires an understanding that it is not enough simply to acknowledge that the universe has the two halves. We say this because there is a third chair occupied by most people in the world who gladly affirm a supernatural aspect of the universe but reject Christianity's very specific and exclusive truth claims. It's accurate to say that most of the people we interact with consider themselves at least open to a form of spirituality in some sense even if they do not subscribe to a particular religious tradition or set of well-defined belief propositions. Yes, skepticism can be rather pervasive in some areas of society, but it is increasingly the case that most share the fundamental intuition that there is something about the universe that is more than just the stuff (the raw ingredients) acted on by fundamental forces.

This is due at least in part to the growing realization of just how lacking is the notion that non-life organized itself into not only living things, but conscious, self-aware persons who wonder about the how and why of it all, seek answers to questions concerning meaning, and long for things such as love, the virtues, and beauty. Not just that it feels off but reducing all about the human experience to nothing more than matter, physics, and energy generating survival-of-the-fittest brain states within our skulls to lack true explanatory power for who and what we are and even what we experience as human beings. Another way to put it is that people have been confronted with the dilemma that accounting for both *why* it is that we seek lives of meaning and *how* to live a meaningful life isn't answerable purely on the basis of objective reality. There is something about these matters that is well beyond merely the mechanics of a physical universe.

In recent years even among the most skeptical of religious belief and practice are becoming more open to the idea that the richness and complexity of our existence is somehow an echo or symptom of a higher reality; something transcendent about the universe that isn't just over and above, but also perhaps even within a person in the form of a soul. Almost everyone has the general sense that they exist as not just some*thing* but some*one*.

I once heard a fairly well-known entertainer relate how being a convinced atheist he had originally rejected any notions attached to mind/body dualism. Yet as he embarked on a personal health and wellness journey, whereby he started feeling better, became happier, nicer, and less judgmental toward others, he came to embrace the notion that the purely organic view of humanity wasn't the complete story. He had a sense that there was a homunculus staring out from behind his eyes driving himself to do things and become a particular kind of person. He characterized it as adopting the view that he was not thinking just with that "lump of matter" in his skull.

This leads to a few questions. What is the center of a person's thought life and overall consciousness if not the brain? Even deeper, what is consciousness and what are thoughts? The Bible's teachings regarding anthropology (what a human being is and what are our characteristics) provide a logically consistent perspective through which to frame these matters. The Christian view is that human beings were created in the image of a personal, communal Being (God as Father, Son, and Holy Spirit) possessing mind, will, and emotions and were endowed with similar personal and relational capacities. And we are best able to thrive when aligning our lives with God's plan for living that touches on all aspects of what it is to be us with the Scriptures being his definitive revelation of how to go about doing so (2 Timothy 3:16-17).

The Christian life then means living in the two halves of reality as defined by the Bible's teachings. And make no mistake, the Bible clearly presents ultimate reality as the interlocking of the material with the spiritual. But it can be a challenge for a Christian to avoid being infiltrated by modern thinking that may discount the spiritual dimension altogether or view it almost as if it is but a rumor of something beyond that isn't to be interacted with or truly experienced moment by moment or even day to day. In fact, we all do this (at least to some extent) at times. I know that I can get immersed in the grind of my day or week and lose sight of what Moses, Kind David, the prophets, Jesus Christ, and the apostles taught and pointed us to in terms of maintaining the proper focus that includes practices that keep me on the right path.

This is helpful to keep in mind since even the most well-meaning Christians can live functionally as if the spiritual dimension as described in the Bible is something just mainly to be believed in and doesn't necessarily take shape in their daily existence. And this can apply even to those who say they believe that the Bible contains absolute truth in both theological and doctrinal issues as well as the historical record that includes spectacular events. If we are not careful, even though we say we are Bible-believing Christians who embrace the supernatural dimension and all that entails, the materialistic or generic spiritualism of our generation can close in on us. It may seep into our thinking without us recognizing it, kind of like a fog creeping in through a window opened only half an inch. When this happens, believers can begin to miss out on the reality of the power of the Christian life.

So, while we say we believe one thing, we allow the spirit of the age to stealthily creep into our thinking and start to take hold. What does the Bible say about how it is that even Christians can lose sight of what is the proper view of the universe and our place in it? Take, for example, Paul's first letter to the church in Corinth, which was a city at the heart of an important trade route in the ancient world. Like many cities that thrived on trade in that era, Corinth had a reputation for sexual immorality, religious diversity, and corruption. The church Paul had spent 18 months building up (Acts 18:1-11) floundered under all these influences and began to divide over various issues.

The heart of the problem in this church was that the world was influencing them rather than they influencing the world. In the opening chapters especially, Paul reminds the Corinthians that the wisdom of God is foolishness to the world, and the wisdom of the world is foolishness to God (1 Corinthians 1:18-25). The Corinthians were not only in the world but also of it, whereas Christ calls believers to be in the world but not of it (John 17:14–19). Christians are called to live in faithful presence among their unbelieving neighbors influencing them with the love of Christ being careful not to conform to worldly patterns of thinking (Romans 12:2). Adhering to Christ's call to be salt and light to a lost world (Matthew 5:13–16) requires living in contrast to the world's fundamental forms and instead adopting the ways of Christ and the apostles (Romans 6:17; 2 Timothy 1:13).

For instance, consider what emerges from the second chapter of Paul's first letter to this church. He makes the claim that his approach in sharing the gospel that led to this church plant taking hold was not based upon flashes of rhetorical brilliance but the basic message of Jesus Christ as crucified validated by demonstrations of the Spirit and the power of God. The "secret and hidden" wisdom Paul and his team imparted was revealed to them through the Holy Spirit who enabled them to both understand and then pass along these truths as those who now should have had a change in mindset (1 Corinthians 2:1-16).

The key point to note in terms of our discussion is how all of this points to a spectacular supernatural reality that starts with Jesus Christ as the divine Son of God—the Word become flesh (John 1:1-3, 14)—who made exclusive truth claims about his identity and mission and what that means for all people. Jesus and the apostles taught that believing in and confessing Christ (John 1:12; Romans 10:9-10) results in a spiritual rebirth (John 3:3; 2 Corinthians 5:17; Titus 3:5; 1 Peter 1:3, 23) whereby a person is forgiven, adopted into God's family as a favored child, and filled with God's Spirit (John 14:15-17; Romans 8:9-11). Again, these are spectacular truth claims regarding what is the nature of ultimate reality with God presiding over and interacting within both the spiritual and material realms in very profoundly personal ways.

Much more could be said about this in light of New Testament teaching but for now it's important to circle back to the idea that even those who accept the whole of Christian teaching can be vulnerable to the influences of the world's mindset, which was precisely what Paul laments throughout his first letter to the Corinthian church. Though Paul and his colleagues were attempting to pass along the gospel as those who "have the mind of Christ" (1 Corinthians 2:16), the members of the church there had to be addressed as "people of the flesh, as infants in Christ" who were not ready for more robust teaching due to their continuing struggles with jealousy, strife, and overall behavior (1 Corinthians 3:1-3).

This underscores how Christians are at risk of losing sight of what the Bible presents as a proper view of the universe by allowing the ceiling that is the naturalistic type of thinking to drop down too low right over our heads. The Bible's view is that the universe consists of both the seen and the unseen, the natural and supernatural; there are those two strands. This means that we must understand, with full intellectual engagement, that we are to live like the universe features these two strands. It comes down to what or who it is that we give ourselves over to in terms of attention and focus that takes shape in what it is that we practice. After all, you get good at whatever it is you practice and if most of my practices are anchored to things of the world rather than the things of God, I shouldn't expect to gain the upper hand in the effort to live well (as defined by God) and prevail in my struggles against sinful inclinations.

We should be willing to ask ourselves the following questions:

- What or who is my primary reference point for not only what to believe but how to think and then live?
- Where do I turn for the prime directives when it comes to how I view myself, the world, and my place in it?

- Where is my focus and attention?

It should come as no surprise to even the most convinced Christian that if you spend most of your time and energy consuming the things of the world that you begin to think and adopt the life patterns as one dominated by the world. It is not complicated! To whatever or whomever I grant time, energy, and focused attention is going to play a major role in what I think and how I live. The Christian is called to submit his mind, will, and emotions (the totality of his being) to seeking God and following Jesus Christ (Matthew 6:19-21, 33; Luke 9:23), which involves developing the proper mindset (Ephesians 4:23; Colossians 3:2). This cannot be done apart from practicing the basic disciplines of prayer, reading and meditating upon the Bible's teachings, and routinely gathering with other believers for worship, encouragement, humble accountability, and service.

If we say we believe wholeheartedly that the God of the Bible exists and that we are in relationship with him by faith in the finished work of Christ on the cross and have his Spirit dwelling within us, then it is going to manifest in our lives. All of this starts with fully embracing as truth the idea that there is a personal God who exists, loves us, and proved it by sending his Son for us. Since that is true, we are to live changed and ever-changing lives!

Chapter 2: The Supernatural Universe (part 2)

Let's push deeper into this with one of the New Testament's more spectacular accounts, the Mount of Transfiguration from the synoptic Gospels (Matthew 17:1-8; Mark 9:2-8; Luke 9:28-36). Here's an actual space-time encounter between Jesus, Moses, and Elijah that was witnessed by three of his followers (Peter, James, and John). We see Jesus having undergone a change in appearance (transfigured) speaking with Moses and Elijah about his coming death in Jerusalem and a voice commanding from out of the cloud, "This is my beloved Son; listen to him! (Mark 9:7)."

This is a preview of Christ in his glory as reigning over the kingdom of God, which is the greater reality a person is pulled into after having trusted Christ as Savior and Lord. It is a foreshadowing of his coming resurrection that makes possible our resurrection as those who will be with him in his kingdom for eternity. This spectacular scene—God the Son having an interaction with legendary figures from ancient times—provides a perspective of reality that is completely at odds with that of the world on a few levels. First, the man who claims to be the Son of God talking with the "ghosts" of recognizable people from centuries ago is enough of a challenge for many. Let's face it, that alone can be a deal-breaker for anyone skeptical of the universe as an open system featuring a supernatural realm. But it goes in another direction as well, which is not quite as apparent at first glance.

The topic of conversation for Moses, Elijah, and Jesus was Christ's coming death. Just before Jesus began his earthly ministry to inaugurate the movement that included both his spectacular truth claims and miraculous feats, he was introduced by John the Baptist who said, "Behold, the Lamb of God, who takes away the sin of the world (John 1:29)." It's easy to miss the fact that by introducing him this way he was directing consideration to Christ's death. How so? For Jews the sacrificial lamb played a central role in the ceremonial observances and rituals that had to do with the cleansing from sin through which a person could be forgiven by and in relationship with God.

So, we have the person who is God in human form talking with Moses and Elijah about his own coming death. Here God, as a true man after the Incarnation, comes as the Lamb of God to take away the sins of the world. This is the very center of the Christian message. Its center is not Christ's life, nor his miracles, but his *death*. This traces all the way back to the very beginning with the pronouncement God made in the Garden.

In Genesis 3:15 we have the first Messianic promise. Continuing in that chapter, we read how evicted humanity is clothed now that he has sinned, which is with the skins of animals that requires the shedding of blood. Then in Genesis 22 we read about the great event that shows Abraham's insight concerning the Messiah who was to come. His one and only son, Isaac, was to be placed on the altar, as a sacrifice—and then a ram is supplied, giving us a double picture of substitution (Isaac as a foreshadowing of an only son being sacrificed as our substitute and then the ram serving to save Isaac as *his* substitute).

This theme continues throughout the centuries in the lead-up to the time of Jesus. In Exodus 12, which was 400 years after the time of Abraham and Isaac, we see the institution of the Passover as a key element of how Abraham's descendants were freed from bondage to Pharaoh's Egypt. This observance included sacrificing a lamb and placing its blood around the doorframe of their homes, which is another foreshadowing of Jesus Christ as the liberating and saving sacrifice. Then around 700 years later (and 700 years before the birth of Jesus) Isaiah prophecies about the coming Messiah and writes of one "despised and rejected...smitten by God, and afflicted...pierced...crushed...cut off out of the land of the living...poured out his soul to death" as the center of the matter (Isaiah 53). These words roll down through the centuries in prophecy after prophecy, and then we come to John the Baptist calling him the Lamb of God. The death of Christ is the subject of thousands of years of prophecy. Again, the center of the Christian message is the redemptive death of Jesus Christ.

So, at the Transfiguration we are brought face-to-face with a supernatural universe with Moses and Elijah speaking to Christ as he is glorified. And we observe that this supernatural universe is not a far-off universe; it was at a particular spot on this planet, at a particular time of the day; there is a perfect continuity with existence as we know it, as in normal life. Then jumping to Christ's redemptive death on the cross, we can say the same thing. The crucifixion of Jesus of Nazareth on that Roman cross would have no true meaning whatsoever outside the relationship of a supernatural world; it's just yet another instance of a religious figure or political zealot crossing the line and getting executed for it. The only reason the term "redemptive death" has any meaning is that there is a personal God who exists and, more than that, has a character. He is not morally neutral. When a man sins against God's character, which is the law of the universe, he is guilty, and God will judge that man on the basis of true moral guilt.

What this highlights is that the true Christian life, as we are examining it, is not to be separated from the Bible's emphasis on the supernatural. This is the Bible's message, and when we see it like this, and are in this framework rather than the naturalistic one or rival spiritualities that can come in so easily upon us, the teachings we're talking about aren't to be dismissed as bizarre. But if we remove the objective reality of the supernatural universe in any area, the great realities of being linked to Jesus in a mystical way resulting in very real and very powerful things immediately falls to the ground. And when that happens, Christianity can be reduced to little more than a psychological and sociological aid as in Aldous Huxley's *Brave New World* or the psychotherapist Carl Jung's interpretation. Religion has a place, not because there is any truth in it, but because man as he is within the evolutionary framework simply needs it; it is what some might refer to as noble fiction that can be good for society in stressing the virtues and even offering certain coping mechanisms for life's distresses.

Yet the fact remains that in our day perhaps the most dangerous threats are the development and spread of rival versions of spirituality that deny the truth as revealed by God through the prophets, Jesus Christ, and the apostles. All the reality of Christianity rests upon the Bible's teachings of the existence of a personal God and a supernatural view of the total universe he created, presides over, and works within that is all centered around the person of Jesus Christ that include his identity, mission, and what he accomplished through his death, resurrection, and ascension. But let's be clear that one is not a Bible-believing Christian in the fullest sense simply by believing the right theological concepts or doctrines, but by living in a manner that harmonizes with what Jesus and the apostles taught about this supernatural world. The Bible teaches that a Christian is living in a supernatural reality now, not only in theory, but in practice.

The Bible does not just speak in abstractions or complex concepts as if it is nothing more than an attempt to arrive at the truth only on the basis of a set of logical arguments; it does not talk about a religious idea far away. It tells about humanity as we are, each person as an individual existing in the universe as it is, which is a personal, supernatural reality. And it tells us how to live in that universe as it is right now.

A helpful passage on what it is to live in light of the supernatural universe is found in 2 Kings 6 where the prophet Elisha and his attendant are surrounded by Syrian forces. Elisha informs the terrified young man that the truth is that there are more on their side than those who are about to attack them, which may have sounded like wishful thinking. Then Elisha prays that his attendant's eyes would be opened, and it became a reality to him. From our standpoint, the significant thing to note here is that the prayer was not that something would come. It was already there. It's just that the young man's eyes had to be opened to see the reality. Think of how often we are like that terrified young fellow who only needed to see with different eyes!

For those who believe that the universe includes the supernatural, these instances and others like it, though spectacular, are instructive, comforting, and perhaps even inspiring all at the same time. Many among us discount the idea that God can intervene in history (including our own personal history) as delusion or fantasy, and the follower of another spiritual tradition tries to recast it. And if the Christian is not careful this mindset can, little by little, take hold and the reality of the supernatural starts slipping away. But the Christian is called to live in the reality of the supernatural. Holding to the right beliefs in terms of theology and doctrine is essential, but there is also to be an experiential reality, moment by moment. And the glory of the experiential is that we can do it with all the intellectual doors wide open.

We aren't just after some spectacular religious experience requiring a dark room, certain types of music, or the influence of hallucinogens; we can know the reality of the supernatural here and now as we are to be in a relationship with God by trusting in the finished work of Jesus Christ on the cross, accepting him as Savior and Lord. The doors are open now—the intellectual doors, and the doors to reality. This is the Christian life, true spirituality. And in light of the Bible's teaching in regard to the supernatural nature of the universe, we are to approach life in all dimensions in a wholehearted trust in Jesus Christ as the crucified and risen Lord who now dwells within us through the Holy Spirit enabling us "to do far more abundantly than all that we ask or think, according to the power at work within us (Ephesians 3:20)..."

Chapter 3: In the Spirit's Power

The Bible presents only two states for the Christian: to be here in the flesh or, having died, to be with the Lord. This is at odds with the view that places the afterlife as an immediate entry into nothingness or being in some shrouded misty place of ethereal formlessness. The Christian is not presented, at the time of death, as being out of contact with sequence, as being nowhere, any more than Jesus is out of contact with sequence or is nowhere between his resurrection and his second coming. Jesus's statement to the thief on the cross that he would be with him in paradise that very day (Luke 23:43) bears this out. And Paul touches on this in 2 Corinthians 5:4-8:

> For while we are still in this tent, we groan, being burdened—not that we would be unclothed, but that we would be further clothed, so that what is mortal may be swallowed up by life. He who has prepared us for this very thing is God, who has given us the Spirit as a guarantee. So we are always of good courage. We know that while we are at home in the body we are away from the Lord, for we walk by faith, not by sight. Yes, we are of good courage, and we would rather be away from the body and

at home with the Lord.

But even stronger than this is Jesus' own words when he had been raised from the dead. When the disciples first encountered the risen Christ, they thought he was a spirit. And this despite the fact that they were supernaturalists, not naturalists; they very much believed in the spiritual realm and perhaps would not have been shocked to have seen a spirit. What they were not prepared for was the physical resurrection. So, in Luke 24:39 we read of Jesus saying to them, "Touch me, and see. For a spirit does not have flesh and bones as you see that I have." He then asks for something to eat to prove to them he was not just a spirit. The proof was not just in seeing, conversing with, or even touching him, but the eating of food right in front of them.

The call to the Christian is not to fear death as if it is a total cessation of being, a disappearance into the void of nothingness, but to realize that at the very moment the body shuts down he will pass into another moment, "today" (like for the dying thief), whatever our today is. That the Christian is immediately with Christ should crush the fear of death for those who have accepted Jesus as Savior. From the Bible's viewpoint this is not given just as a psychological hope. The dead are really there in a conscious state with Jesus. They are there. It is as much a part of the total universe as you are sitting here reading this. It's not in some philosophic "other," but in reality. Time is important. The thief was not there until he got there.

The Bible teaches that there are two equal lines of reality presented to us. We are in the seen world and there are also Christians who have died, who are with Christ now. This is the biblical view of truth: there are two strands of space-time reality with one in the seen, and one in the unseen. Therefore I am to live now by faith, grounded in three space-time realities: what has occurred, such as Christ's death and resurrection; what exists right now in the unseen realm including my loved ones who had accepted Christ as Savior and died and are now with him in an actual place; and what is to come, including my future bodily resurrection and return with Christ.

This should inspire us to live in a manner reflecting an authentic and expectant hope that takes shape in having a more joyous and tranquil outlook no matter the particular circumstances we experience. The gospel provides the animating principles for how best to be the creatures God made us to be: human beings bearing his image. And we are presented with the calling to be this creature by choice, to bow in our will and live intentionally as followers of Jesus Christ, which he said involves a daily pattern of self-denial and bearing the weight of God's authority upon all aspects of your life. Christians are to integrate what they believe about God, Christ, and ourselves as adopted children—all of which is taught in the Bible—into every dimension of living.

And this is where we get into the practicality of it all. How is it possible to live this way? All this talk of the Christian life and spirituality, which is basically the ideals taught and exemplified by Christ and the apostles, is often quite daunting and can feel out of reach. How are we to live this way, if we are to think of this not merely as some sort of abstract religious experience, a set of unattainable ideals, a combination of mood and moment, a vague, meaningless existential experience? How do I get started? Is it in forms of asceticism, which is an intentional forsaking of certain pleasures or imposing forms of suffering upon the self, or through ecstatic, even exotic, experiences? The answer to all these is no. The Bible doesn't give this to us as just some kind of religious idea that includes mechanical observances but an intensely practical one.

Let's go back to the passage in 2 Corinthians 5 and take special note of verses 4-5:

> For while we are still in this tent, we groan, being burdened—not that we would be unclothed, but that we would be further clothed, so that what is mortal may be swallowed up by life. He who has prepared us for this very thing

is God, who has given us the Spirit as a guarantee.

We see here God drawing two factors of reality together: our being with Christ when we die, and at the present time with equal certainty, we who have accepted Christ as Savior have the very Spirit of God dwelling within us. These two elements are not to be thought of separately. When I die it is certain that I will be with the Lord. Those who have trusted Christ and have gone before us are there with him this very instant. But at the same time, in this moment, I have the Holy Spirit living within me.

So, when Jesus told the thief he would that day be with him in paradise he meant it. That applies to me as well in my life and in this time. For me to die is to immediately be with the Lord. It is not just an idea; it is a reality. But at the same time, Christ gives the promise just as definitely that when I have accepted him as my Savior, he lives in me. *They are equal reality.* These are two streams of present reality, both equally promised. Christ through the Holy Spirit really lives in me!

The Christ who was crucified—whose work is finished and who is now glorified—has promised to bring forth fruit in the Christian just as the sap of the vine brings forth fruit in the branch. In the Gospel of John, the apostle records Jesus as saying, "I am the vine; you are the branches. Whoever abides in me and I in him, he it is that bears much fruit, for apart from me you can do nothing (John 15:5)." There we have it. Connected to the glorified Christ by faith, which is a wholehearted trust in him, that results in his Spirit living within and enabling a person to live, speak, think, and even desire in the ways that lead to flourishing as the image-bearers of God we were created to be.

Note what Jesus' half-brother James wrote in his letter: "Of his own will he brought us forth by the word of truth, that we should be a kind of firstfruits of his creatures (James 1:18)." The Bible teaches that by grace through faith a person enters into a mystical union with Jesus Christ in order to bring forth fruit into the external world.

Three points to keep in mind moving forward. First concerns the how. It is not, nor can it be, done simply in our own strength. Us bearing the fruit as a connected branch has one active ingredient: The glorified Christ will be the one doing it through us.

This brings us to the second point, which is the agency of the Holy Spirit. In Romans we read, "and hope does not put us to shame, because God's love has been poured into our hearts through the Holy Spirit who has been given to us (Romans 5:5)." One application from this truth is that Christians do not have to wallow in shame when we struggle and blow it. The reality of our current existence in a fallen realm includes our own inclinations still pulling us to conform to the world and the self as central. That said, we have to be careful not to fall into adopting a casual view of sin in our lives. Yes, the Bible doesn't teach that we're ever going to be perfect in this life, but we are taught to lament our sin such that we do not stay comfortable with patterns of living that are contrary to God's plan. Lament and repent; feeling the weight of our sin should lead us to course correct as needed as Paul wrote in 2 Corinthians 7:10: "For godly grief (sorrow) produces a repentance that leads to salvation without regret, whereas worldly grief (sorrow) produces death."

Our experience echoes the examples of those throughout the Bible who also experienced the unrelenting struggle to move against the grain of the world around us and our own desires. Indeed, the struggle is real, but we have the promise that God's love is "poured out into our hearts through the Holy Spirt" so we don't have to feel ashamed to the point of giving in to despair. When we fall, we can get up off the ground and back on the path following Christ.

> Hebrews 4:15-16 For we do not have a high priest who is unable to sympathize with our weaknesses, but one who in every respect has been tempted as we are, yet without sin. Let us then with

confidence draw near to the throne of grace, that we may receive mercy and find grace to help in time of need.

But back to the practicality of what it is to live as a Christian in light of the supernatural reality. Paul writes in Romans 7:6, "But now we are released from the law, having died to that which held us captive, so that we serve in the new way of the Spirit and not in the old way of the written code." The difference in all of this is that the Holy Spirit—a Person, not just an idea—has been given to us to do a work within and through us. *It is not to be in our own strength.* Later in that same letter, Paul writes "For if you live according to the flesh you will die, but if by the Spirit you put to death the deeds of the body, you will live (Romans 8:13)."

The Holy Spirit is specifically identified here (chapter 8 is one of the central passages in all the Bible in regard to the work of the Holy Spirit) as the agent of the power and person of the glorified Christ. There is not enough strength in ourselves, but the power and work of the glorified Christ is operational within us by the agency of the Holy Spirit. This is what Christ meant when he said: "I will not leave you as orphans; I will come to you (John 14:18)."

Our third point is that this does not represent a passivity on our part as if our will, intention, and desire to carry out the Lord's commands aren't involved in our moment to moment lives.

A prime illustration of this is Mary's response to the angel that we read in Luke's Gospel account. The angel tells her she is to give birth to the long-promised Messiah, which is a unique and unrepeatable occurrence: the birth of the second Person of the Trinity into this world. The Holy Spirit is to cause a conception in her womb. She could have said, "I do not want to be that person. I want to remove myself from consideration; I decline; I want out of this. What would Joseph and my family say?" She could have also said, "I now have these amazing promises, so I will exert my force, my character, and my energy, to bring forth this amazing promise. I have the promise. Now I will bring forth a child without the need of a man." But that response would never have worked since she could not bring forth a child without a man by her own will, any more than any other woman could.

But there was a third thing she could say, which is wonderful. She says, "Behold, I am the servant of the Lord; let it be to me according to your word (Luke 1:38)." There is the active passivity we have talked about. She took her own body, by choice, and put it into the hands of God to do the thing that he said he would do, and Jesus was born. She gave herself, with her body, to God. In response to the promise, yes; but not to do it herself. This is a beautiful, exciting, personal expression of a relationship between a finite person and the God she loves. Now this is absolutely unique and must not be confused; there is only one Virgin Birth. Nevertheless, it is an illustration of our being the bride of Christ.

We are in a similar situation in that we have these amazing and thrilling promises we have been considering, and we are neither to think of ourselves as totally passive, as if we have no part in this, nor that we can do it ourselves. If we are to bear fruit in the Christian life by the agency of the Holy Spirit (it's not us doing it, but him), faith must be acted on consistently by adopting the following mindset: *On the basis of your promises I am looking for you to fulfill them, Lord Jesus; bring forth your fruit through me into this world.*

So now we stand before two streams of reality for Christians: those who have passed and are with Christ now; and we who live now and have, because of the finished work of Christ, access to his power—not in theory, but in reality—by the agency of the Holy Spirit. Christian spirituality is not achieved by our own efforts using our own energy. The "how" of this life is summed up in Romans 6:11: "...consider yourselves dead to sin and alive to God in Christ Jesus." Count yourselves (there is the faith) dead to sin (there is the negative aspect) but alive to God (the positive aspect) in Christ Jesus. This is the "how," and there is no other way. It is the power of the crucified, risen, and gloried Christ, through the agency of the Holy Spirit by faith as we engage our heart, mind, and will to follow him. This is Christian spirituality.

Chapter 4: Life in the Church

Since the Fall there have been two humanities, and not just one. There are those who are still in rebellion against God, and there are those who by God's grace have returned to him on the basis of Christ's work on the cross. The church should be the reality and the exhibition of this distinction. Not a distinction as in we are, as those in Christ, better *than* others but the better for it and live in a manner that reflects that fact.

The Bible teaches that the church is, in a very special sense, the body of Christ (Ephesians 5). And as his body, the church should exhibit him to the world. Just as our bodies are our means of communication to the world around us, so the church as the body of Christ should be one of the chief means he communicates to the external world. Another way to frame this is to recognize how we think our thoughts and then convey them to the world through our bodies; our physical body is the point of communication with the external world, and this is the way we affect the world. So, the church, as the body of Jesus Christ, is called to be the means whereby he may be exhibited to and act within the world until he comes again. Every single generation should be able to look to the church of that generation and see an exhibition of a supernaturally restored relationship, not just between the individual and God, though that is first; not just between the individual and himself, though that is crucial; but between people in the church.

The word "church" comes from a Greek word that means "a gathering of those who have been called." It has to do with being called out of a lost humanity into a new tribe, a new family of people from every conceivable background forming a community of those whose lives are centered on God through faith in Christ. That is the calling of the church.

Everywhere you turn people have the sense that we are less than we know we should be. Our generation sees this, but the problem is not new. Ever since the Fall, rebellious man has been this way and senses that things are somehow not in the proper order; something is off or out of joint. And the church is called out of this humanity in order to be a united humanity before a lost humanity.

As I am living individually in a supernatural universe there should be individual results, and an individual display. But equally, living as a collective body made up of many people in light of the supernatural reality of God at work among those he has called, there will be results and a display of them in a collective sense. It is not only that the individual should so think and live, but the whole group as a community should be attuned to living consciously in the reality of the supernatural. Then there is the witness, the display that should occur.

This is a high calling, a special oneness in Christians moving and working together—a unity that is not merely organizational or in some abstract sense. It will not be perfect, because the Bible never says we're going to be perfect in this life, but on the basis of what Jesus Christ has done there should be a substantially restored relationship among Christians here and now, which has immediate practical implications. First, in exhibiting who God is, as he has revealed himself generally through the natural order and specially by direct communications with mediators who have given us the Bible, there must therefore be an emphasis on the truth about what is most real. God exists, God created the universe and human beings in his image for the purposes of knowing him, loving him, and obeying him. Human beings have rebelled against this, and we are all caught up in it. And God's plan of redemption and restoration of what became a fractured relationship converges on the message (the gospel) that Jesus Christ has taken upon himself what is necessary for there to be a restored relationship. So, the first exhibition of the church has to do with making known what is ultimately true.

For if the church is not holding to and declaring the truths God has revealed, then the body is telling lies about its Head. There is truth to be known that is knowable and Christians are to share the message. This sharing must be in words, but our actions must then back up those words. We must live in a manner consistent with the message we are boldly proclaiming. Otherwise, the world has no reason to believe they are true. The church is not a group of people that merely thinks up ideas; the church is to be a declarative statement of what God has revealed concerning himself and us in the Bible.

So, all these propositional aspects, as in what is true about God's nature and our nature and that sin is a moral issue that stands between us and God, are established by God himself. The church as a group of people joining together across every conceivable social divide represents the supernaturally restored human race in reality when we conduct ourselves as the family of forgiven and adopted children we are meant to be.

Though we cannot, individually and as the church, exhibit God's full character perfectly in this life, we are called to reflect the fact that he is personally involved with us as we walk by faith in the truth of the finished work of Christ on the cross that results in his Spirit empowering us. That said, the battle against false doctrine and sin will never end in this life, which means that there do exist legal aspects of our relationship with the God who is there. But the proper legal relationship having to do with right beliefs that include acknowledging our sin and need for a Savior is only the entryway into the reality of a personal relationship with God as Father. And once in that relationship, which is as an adopted child (John 1:12; Romans 8:15; Ephesians 1:5; 1 John 3:1), we are then connected to his other children—those in the church.

Being in relationship with God, to enjoy him and manifest aspects of his character in our own lives, can never be simply mechanical or perfunctory but must also be deeply personal. This is what leads to a display of redeemed human personal relationships that takes the shape of the kinship of believers that the Apostles Creed refers to as the "communion of saints." There is a mystical union of believers that is to be clearly displayed to the world. When I put my trust in Jesus Christ and am born again into a new life, I come into a new relationship with the God who created the universe and become a brother to all other Christians in the family of God. It is meant to be a true kinship that is a demonstration of God's existence and Jesus Christ as risen Savior and King.

What should the church consciously and consistently be then? The church should be that which encourages its members in the true Christian life, in proper spirituality. It should encourage them to walk in freedom in the present life as those throwing off the chains sin wraps around us. It should encourage substantial healing in their separation from themselves and a substantial healing in their separation from their neighbor, especially fellow Christians. To do these things, the church must first teach the truth, and second, the church should teach what it is to practice the reality of and be an expression of God's character; that of holiness and love. The church cannot merely teach these things in words; we must see the practice of these things in the church as a corporate body.

Can faith be taught? Yes, but not just in the words of theological and doctrinal orthodoxy, but most completely by a life lived in a manner that reflects the teachings. You cannot teach faith only as an abstraction or merely a set of belief propositions. There must be a demonstration of the Christian life in word and action if it is to be learned and then lived out.

We are called, individually and as the church, to function moment by moment by conscious choice on the basis of the work of Christ through the power of the Holy Spirit, by faith. We must also teach in words the duty to exhibit that God exists and that he is personal, and practice as a corporate body what Jesus and the apostles taught and exemplified. We must also, in words and practice, show that the church takes holiness and love expressed toward others seriously. And how can we do this unless consciously, intentionally, and diligently extending love and compassion toward fellow believers as well as those outside the church?

If the church as a body made up of all the individual parts (each person being a vital part of the body) does not consciously seek freedom from sin's power, because of the finished work of Christ in the power of the Spirit by faith, how can we teach these things with integrity in mere words?

In light of this challenge, the church's methods are very important. They must be done with the conscious awareness of the supernatural nature of reality. We must function as though the supernatural is there, that we exist in a universe where the natural and supernatural are an interlocking reality; there is no escaping this truth for one who reads and takes seriously the Bible. So, what are we to do about it but to exhibit the supernatural to our generation? And part of this involves not just the message of Christ but declaring it in the way the Lord would have us do so.

There must be something the world cannot merely explain away on the basis of its methods or by applied psychology. And I am not speaking here of the special manifestations of the Holy Spirit, but the normal and universal promise to the church concerning the Spirit's work that enables us to love well, forgive, cooperate, and do things for our neighbors that make a difference in their lives and the communities we're in. Though we do not routinely display truly miraculous manifestations of God's Spirit in our daily interactions with those in our lives, we can exemplify the character of Christ to everyone, both believers and non-believers. Blessing as opposed to cursing; mercy and forgiveness as opposed to revenge; kindness, compassion, and sacrifice as opposed to callousness and selfishness; generosity as opposed to greed and materialism. This is how the world sees evidence that God exists, and that the gospel of Jesus Christ is true. Having accepted Christ as Savior, we are to live and walk in the power of God's Spirit within us with the fruit of doing so to serve as authentication that the message is true.

These are the things an unbelieving world should see when they look at the church—something that they cannot easily explain away. The church should be committed to the practical reality of these things, not merely agreeing to them. In a fallen world there is need of organization, and there is also need of Christian leadership. But the leaders, as office-bearers, stand in relationship to the church, to the people of God, as brothers and sisters in Christ as well as leaders. The church as a whole, and those in leadership, are to function consciously on the basis of each one being equal as created in the image of God, and as equal in the sense of being sinners redeemed by the blood of Jesus. In this way, believing in the priesthood of all true believers (1 Peter 2:9), believing in the supernaturally restored relationship among those who are brothers and sisters in Christ, believing in the indwelling of the Holy Spirit in each individual Christian, we are able to stand together in accordance with Christian spirituality.

The local church must be right doctrinally, but it should also be a beautiful example of the supernatural that includes the substantially healed relationship in this present life between people. If there is no reality of this, we deny what we say we believe, right up to the apex of our belief system, because what we really deny is that God is a personal God who acts upon and within those in relationship with him through faith in Jesus Christ. There must be the mindset of a genuine interest in people as people, and not just as church members, attenders, fellow workers, or givers.

The environment of the local church must be conducive to the growth in all personal relationships. This requires teaching and exemplifying the present meaning of the work of Christ, and a conscious choice of the individual and the group to lay hold of these things and help one another to put them into practice. The church is to function consciously on the basis of Christ's work and the supernaturally restored relationship between God and those who have trusted Christ, and not in our natural gifts and talents. The Holy Spirit is the one by whom the body is joined together (Ephesians 4:15-17) and empowered to love one another in the manner of and as commanded by Jesus, as well as to go and make disciples as we reach out and extend love to the community. This is the Christian life. This is Christian spirituality.

Chapter 5: The Christian and the Law(s)

In conclusion, following are questions I should ask myself in regard to my Christian walk:

- Am I exemplifying what I say I believe and should be the result of the gospel?
- Do I resemble what it is to be one who is more and more resembling the one I say I am following? (e.g., Matthew 11:29; Romans 12:9-21; Philippians 2:1-4; 1 John 2:5-6)
- Why does it seem to be so hard to successfully live out the Christian life?

The challenges associated with the above questions can be traced to a lack of understanding of what the Bible says about the meaning of the finished work of Christ for our present lives. In other words, at the root of our struggle is a disconnect between what the Bible teaches about this and how we live moment by moment.

What are the fundamental elements of the gospel?

1. God exists, God is personal, and God is holy; God's character as a Person who is holy is the law of the universe (Leviticus

11:45; Isaiah 6:3; Hebrews 11:6; 1 Peter 1:16; Revelation 4:8). God's personality (His being a Person) is the very basis for human relationship and communication. The sense or intuition that almost all human beings share that there is something about the universe that is not only transcendent but that somehow connects us is because God as a Person has created a universe that is personal and not in a pantheistic (or even panentheistic) sense (Psalm 19:1-6; Ecclesiastes 3:11; Acts 14:17; Romans 1:19-20, 2:14-15).

2. People are separated from God on the basis of their true moral guilt as transgressors of God's law. And that guilt is not just a psychological guilty feeling in a person but moral guilt before the infinite, personal, holy God (Romans 3:9, 23; Galatians 3:22; James 4:4).

3. The Bible teaches that only the finished, substitutionary work of Christ upon the cross as the sacrificial Lamb of God—in history, in space and time—is enough to remove this guilt. Our true guilt stands between us and God and can be removed only upon the basis of the finished work of Christ. We cannot do anything to remove or atone for that guilt. Just as the only basis for the removal of our guilt is the finished work of Christ upon the cross, so the only instrument for accepting that finished

work is faith (Romans 3:20-26, 8:1-4; Ephesians 2:1-9; Colossians 2:11-15).
4. The moment we place our trust in Jesus Christ as Savior we pass from being spiritually dead to spiritually alive; from the kingdom of darkness to God's kingdom (Colossians 1:12-14; Titus 3:5-7). That is what Jesus and the apostles refer to as being born again, experiencing the new birth. There is no way to begin the Christian life except through the door of this spiritual birth, any more than there is any other way to begin physical life except through the door of a physical birth discounting artificial means that may emerge as something outside the normal flow of how a human being enters into the world (John 3:3-8; 2 Corinthians 5:17; 1 Peter 1:3, 23).

But birth is just the beginning of a new life! The important thing after being born is to live, both physically and spiritually. There is a new birth, and then there is the Christian life to be lived. This is not to be done mechanically as if it all boils down to lists of things to do and not do. However, we also must not dismiss the fact that prescriptions in the form of lists do exist that God has instituted and given to us for our good with the chief being the Ten Commandments (Exodus 20:1-17) and the Law of Love (Mark 12:30-31).

Now about the Ten Commandments. The climax of that list is the tenth (Exodus 20:17): "You shall not covet...anything that is your neighbor's," which is a completely inward thing. Coveting is a form of desire (not all of which is sinful) that becomes sin when it fails to include love of God or love of my fellow man. Two practical tests come into view here; first, I am to love God enough to be contented (Proverbs 3:5-6; Philippians 4:11-13; 1 Timothy 6:6-8; Hebrews 13:5); second, I am to love my neighbor enough not to envy.

It is fascinating that this is the last of the Ten Commandments yet it is the hub of the whole thing. The end of the entire list of commandments is that we arrive at an inward situation. In fact, we break this last commandment before we break any of the others. Any time we break one of the other commandments of God, it means we have coveted. It also means that any time we break one of the others, we break this one as well.

Paul underscores this when he writes in Romans 7:7-9: "What then shall we say? That the law is sin? By no means! Yet if it had not been for the law, I would not have known sin. For I would not have known what it is to covet if the law had not said, 'You shall not covet.' But sin, seizing an opportunity through the commandment, produced in me all kinds of covetousness. For apart from the law, sin lies dead. I was once alive apart from the law, but when the commandment came, sin came alive and I died."

It's worth noting that not all desires having to do with improving one's position in the various aspects of life (professionally, academically, financially, relationally, etc.) rise to the level of discontentment that crosses over into coveting. It is more concerned with an attitude of thankfulness and submission to the Lord in any given moment such that desires for things of the world not dominate our thinking and result in actions that are contrary to God's blueprint for living.

Think of the first instance of this. How does coveting emerge in the Garden? Instead of keeping the things of God foremost in their thinking and being thankful to God for what they did have, Adam and Eve's longings became compromised with the result being death and chaos. The Bible teaches that the Fall had lasting effects that all human beings have endured with Jesus Christ being the lone human who was caught up in it only in the sense of being the sacrifice to provide the possibility of redemption and restoration. And for those who put their trust in Christ—confess him as Savior and Lord—God the Father is our Father and God's Spirit moves within us to empower us to live well.

What does it mean to live well within this context? We have established that the inward area is the first battleground of the Christian life (coveting is an inward thing) with inner attitudes, mindsets, and matters of the heart resulting in outward acts. The internal is basic, the external is always merely the result. This truth is critical to take hold of as our starting place in the effort to live as Christians. We will never be perfect in this life, but the possibility exists that we can walk more closely aligned with what Jesus and the apostles taught and exemplified as documented in the Bible.

Let's summarize what we've covered with some concluding thoughts. The true Christian life does not just mean that we have been born again, are justified, and are destined for heaven. It must begin there, but it means much more than that. The call of Jesus Christ is to deny self, take up a cross daily, and follow him, which is an act of the will to abandon one life in favor of another (Luke 9:23-24). It is acknowledging and embracing God's prescriptions for living that include the whole of the Ten Commandments and the Law of Love, which starts in the realm of our thoughts as the intent to not covet against God and other people.

The Christian life is a positive approach to doing things as opposed to the negative of not doing certain things. And this positivity begins with the inward reality that then manifests in outward results. The positive inward reality of the new birth and presence of the Spirit of God within a person who has accepted Christ as Savior flows into the external world of behavior and speech, which is what it is to submit to Christ as Lord on a moment-by-moment basis. We are not just dead to certain things, but we are alive to a God we love and are in relationship with him as a person who is there. And we are to love others and relate to them as fellow image-bearers of God with all that this entails.

This necessarily involves practicing the fundamental spiritual disciplines:

- Reading, contemplating, and putting into practice the Bible's teachings and commandments.
- Praying in accordance with the teachings and examples of Christ, the apostles, and the prophets.
- Gathering with other Christians for worship, the mutual building up of one another, accountability, and service (both within the church and in the community).

This is what it is to work *out* (not for) your salvation knowing that the Lord is at work within you to enable you to live a life pleasing to him (Philippians 2:12-13). This is Christian spirituality that leads to living for Jesus every moment.

About the Author

Johnny is author of *A Thought-out Faith: Christianity as the Best Explanation*, an ordained pastor, keynote speaker at various civic, business and church events/functions, board member of two non-profit organizations, and holds a health coach certification through the American Council on Exercise. He lives with his wife, Jill, in the northern Virginia/Washington, DC area where they serve in their church together and stay active in the lives of their three sons and their families. If interested in having Johnny appear as a guest speaker/presenter at your event he can be reached at johnnyarm77@gmail.com.

www.ingramcontent.com/pod-product-compliance
Lightning Source LLC
Chambersburg PA
CBHW061257040426
42444CB00010B/2399